The · Life Cycle · Series

The Life Cycle of a

BEAVER

Bobbie Kalman

Crabtree Publishing Company

www.crabtreebooks.com

The Life Cycle Series
A Bobbie Kalman Book

Dedicated by Michael Hodge
To my wonderful wife Jenn. I love you.

Author and Editor-in-Chief
Bobbie Kalman

Writing team
Bobbie Kalman
Larissa Kostoff
Kathryn Smithyman

Substantive editor
Kathryn Smithyman

Project editor
Michael Hodge

Editors
Molly Aloian
Kelley MacAulay

Design
Margaret Amy Salter
Samantha Crabtree (cover)

Production coordinator
Heather Fitzpatrick

Photo research
Crystal Foxton

Consultant
Patricia Loesche, Ph.D., Animal Behavior Program,
Department of Psychology, University of Washington

Illustrations
Barbara Bedell: page 4 (capybara)
Vanessa Parson-Robbs: back cover, pages 4 (jerboa), 6, 9, 11, 14, 17, 28, 30
Margaret Amy Salter: pages 18-19, 22-23

Photographs
Alan & Sandy Carey/Alpha Presse: page 16
Animals Animals - Earth Scenes: © Loomis, Jennifer: page 27; © Whitehead, Fred:
    page 29 (top)
Bruce Coleman Inc.: Jen & Des Bartlett: pages 11, 12; Erwin & Peggy Bauer:
    page 13 (top); Wolfgang Bayer: page 8 (top); Norman Owen Tomalin: page 7 (bottom)
© W. Perry Conway/Corbis: page 25
iStockphoto.com: pages 20, 26, 29 (bottom), 30
Minden Pictures: Konrad Wothe: page 31 (top)
Photo Researchers, Inc.: Tom & Pat Leeson: front cover, page 10; James Steinberg: page 21
robertmccaw.com: pages 13 (bottom), 24
© ShutterStock.com/Robert Kyllo: page 28
Visuals Unlimited: Bill Banaszewski: page 17; John Green: page 5; William Grenfell:
    pages 14-15
Other images by Corel, Creatas, and Photodisc

Library and Archives Canada Cataloguing in Publication

Kalman, Bobbie, date.
    The life cycle of a beaver / Bobbie Kalman

(The Life cycle series)
Includes index.
ISBN-13: 978-0-7787-0628-1 (bound)
ISBN-13: 978-0-7787-0702-8 (pbk.)
ISBN-10: 0-7787-0628-1 (bound)
ISBN-10: 0-7787-0702-4 (pbk.)
    1. Beavers--Life cycles--Juvenile literature. I. Title. II. Series.

QL737.R632K34 2006   j599.37   C2006-904119-9

Library of Congress Cataloging-in-Publication Data

Kalman, Bobbie.
    The life cycle of a beaver / Bobbie Kalman.
       p. cm. -- (The Life Cycle series)
    ISBN-13: 978-0-7787-0628-1 (rlb)
    ISBN-10: 0-7787-0628-1 (rlb)
    ISBN-13: 978-0-7787-0702-8 (pb)
    ISBN-10: 0-7787-0702-4 (pb)
    1. Beavers--Life cycles--Juvenile literature. I. Title. II. Series.

QL737.R632K355 2007
599.37--dc22
                                                    2006023330

Crabtree Publishing Company

www.crabtreebooks.com   1-800-387-7650

Published in Canada
Crabtree Publishing
616 Welland Ave.
St. Catharines, ON
L2M 5V6

Published in the United States
Crabtree Publishing
PMB16A
350 Fifth Ave., Suite 3308
New York, NY 10118

Published in the United Kingdom
Crabtree Publishing
White Cross Mills
High Town, Lancaster
LA1 4XS

Published in Australia
Crabtree Publishing
386 Mt. Alexander Rd.
Ascot Vale (Melbourne)
VIC 3032

Contents

What are beavers?

Beavers are **mammals**. Mammals are **warm-blooded** animals. The bodies of warm-blooded animals stay about the same temperatures in both hot and cold places. Mammals have **backbones**. They also have body parts called **lungs** for breathing air. Baby mammals **nurse**, or drink milk from the bodies of their mothers.

The capybara is the largest rodent in the world. It can grow to be over four feet (1 m) long!

The thick-tailed pygmy jerboa is the smallest rodent in the world. It grows to be only 2 inches (5 cm) long! The jerboa's tail is more than twice as long as its body.

Long-toothed mammals

Beavers belong to a group of mammals called **rodents**. Capybaras, squirrels, mice, and jerboas are other kinds of rodents. Rodents have long teeth. Their teeth never stop growing. Rodents **gnaw**, or constantly chew, on hard objects using their teeth. Gnawing helps stop their teeth from growing too long. It also helps keep their teeth sharp.

Two kinds of beavers

There are two **species**, or types, of beavers—the American beaver and the Eurasian beaver. The American beaver lives throughout most of North America. The Eurasian beaver lives in many countries in northern Europe and northern Asia. This book is about the American beaver.

Beaver habitats

Beavers live in forests. Forests are their **habitats**. A habitat is the natural place where an animal lives. Within their habitats, beavers make homes called **lodges** in streams, rivers, ponds, and lakes. The beavers use the trees that surround these waterways to make their lodges.

Beavers build lodges only in water that is at least four feet (1 m) deep. The water must also be slow-moving water so that it will not wash away the lodges.

5

Beaver bodies

A beaver's body is suited to life in water. A beaver has thick, **waterproof** fur. It also has a long, flat tail. It uses its tail to steer and to **propel**, or push, its body forward in water. The toes on a beaver's **hind**, or back, paws are **webbed**. Webbed toes have thin skin between them. Paws with webbed toes are like flippers. They help beavers propel themselves through water.

A beaver's tail is long, flat, and shaped like the end of a paddle. It is covered with tough skin.

*A beaver's long front teeth are called **incisors**. They are covered with tough, bright-orange **enamel**.*

*A beaver has **castors**, or scent glands, under the base of its tail.*

*A beaver has **split claws** on its hind paws. It uses these claws to comb its fur while it **grooms**, or cleans, itself.*

A beaver has five toes on each of its front paws. Each toe has a sharp claw.

6

Fabulous fur

A beaver has two layers of fur on its body. There is a thick layer of soft fur, called **underfur**, next to the beaver's skin. The underfur keeps the beaver's body warm. The outer layer of fur is made up of long, thick hairs called **guard hairs**. The beaver grooms itself to keep its guard hairs clean and waterproof. The layer of waterproof guard hairs keeps the beaver's underfur and skin dry.

*When the weather gets colder in autumn, a beaver's fur gets thicker. Thick fur keeps the beaver warm in cold weather. When the weather warms up in spring, the beaver **molts**, or sheds, some of this fur.*

Good grooming

A beaver grooms itself often. It begins to groom by scrubbing its face, belly, and shoulders with its front paws. It combs the rest of its fur using the split claws on its hind paws. The beaver has **oil glands** under the base of its tail. Using its front paws, it spreads oil from the oil glands over its body. The oil coats the guard hairs, making them waterproof. It also makes the fur slick. Having slick fur helps the beaver glide through water.

This beaver is grooming itself.

What is a life cycle?

Life span

A life cycle is not the same as a **life span**. A life span is the length of time an animal is alive. A beaver's life span is between ten and twenty years. The oldest known beaver lived to be 21.

All animals go through a set of changes called a **life cycle**. Early in its life cycle, an animal hatches from an egg or is born. The animal changes over time until it is an adult. An adult animal can **mate**, or join together with another animal of the same species to make babies. With each baby, a new life cycle begins.

The life cycle of a beaver

Beaver **embryos**, or developing babies, grow inside their mother's body until they are ready to be born. In spring, **kits**, or baby beavers, are born in a group called a **litter**. There are usually four kits in a litter. The kits live in the lodge with both of their parents. The next spring, the young beavers are **yearlings**, or one-year-old beavers. At this time, the mother beaver has another litter. The lodge now contains about ten beavers—the mother, the father, four yearlings, and four kits. This family group is called a **colony**. The yearlings live in the lodge until the following spring, when they are two. Two-year-old beavers are called **juveniles**. Each juvenile leaves the lodge to find a **partner**. By winter, the juveniles are adults. Each pair of adults creates its own colony by mating and having kits. The beaver partners will stay together for the rest of their lives.

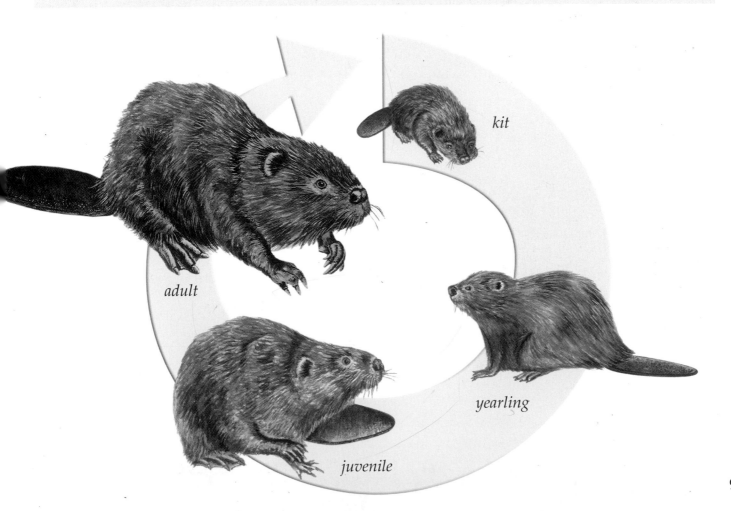

kit

adult

yearling

juvenile

The kits are born

Most beaver kits are born in April, May, or early
June. Each newborn kit weighs about one pound
(0.5 kg) and is around twelve inches (30 cm) long.
Kits are born with fur on their bodies. After
the kits are born, the mother beaver grooms
their fur. The kits begin to nurse immediately.

When kits are born, their fur is red, brown, or black. The kits stay with their parents for about two years.

10

Parent care

Both the mother and the father beavers take care of the kits. They groom the kits often. Kits have incisors poking through their gums. When the kits are about three days old, they begin to eat plant foods. The parents carry leaves and soft twigs into the lodge. They hold this food in their mouths so the kits can nibble on it. The kits continue to nurse for at least another month, however.

Safe inside

Many kits are able to swim soon after they are born, but adult beavers usually keep them inside the lodge. In the lodge, the kits are safe from **predators**. Predators are animals that hunt and eat other animals. Wolves, bears, and eagles are some animals that eat kits.

Kits squeal and cry for food and attention from their parents.

Getting bigger

This mother beaver is helping one of her kits get back into the lodge after a swim.

By the time the kits are two weeks old, their parents have taught them how to groom themselves. This lesson is important for beavers! As the kits groom, they keep their bodies clean and healthy and make their fur waterproof.

Active at night

Beavers are **nocturnal** animals. Nocturnal animals are active mainly at night. When the kits are about three weeks old, they go on their first nighttime swims.

Dive in

As the kits learn to swim, their parents watch them closely. Some kits can swim well immediately, whereas others hang on to a parent's back or tail. A parent may carry a kit in its mouth if the kit cannot swim well. Before long, all the kits can swim on their own.

Finding their own food

When kits are three months old, they stop nursing. The kits are now strong swimmers, so they can **forage**, or search for food, on their own. They eat leaves and bark. Using their teeth, they strip the bark from the branches of **saplings**, or small trees. The food helps the kits grow quickly. By the time kits are four months old, they weigh ten pounds (4.5 kg)!

Two-month-old kits, such as the one above, spend more time outside the lodge than they did when they were younger. They still stay near their parents, however.

Learning by helping

Kits learn everything they need to know by copying their parents. They carry tree branches back to the lodge, as shown right. The beavers use some of the branches for food. They use other branches to repair the lodge. They place the branches on the outside of the lodge and then cover them with mud. In autumn, the entire beaver family works together to repair the lodge. These repairs keep the lodge warm and dry in winter.

Yearlings

At twelve months of age, young beavers are called yearlings. They have grown a lot in one year, but they are not yet fully grown. Yearlings continue to live in the lodge with their parents. They spend a lot of time foraging for food. They work together with their parents, helping repair the lodge or add to it.

Babysitters

Once the young beavers are yearlings, their mother has another litter of kits. The yearlings sometimes gather around their mother while she gives birth to the kits. Yearlings help their parents care for the kits. They gather food for the kits, groom them, and play with them.

Leaving home

Two-year-old beavers leave the lodge in spring. They are now juveniles. After leaving the lodge, the juveniles do not stay together. Each juvenile swims **downstream**, following the direction in which the water flows.

The search is on!

A juvenile swims downstream looking for two things—a partner and a **territory** in which to live. A territory is the area in which a beaver—or a colony of beavers—lives and finds food. The juvenile finds a partner that is a juvenile of the opposite sex. Some juveniles find partners first, and then they look for a territory together. Other juveniles find territories first, and then they wait for partners to join them. Once a juvenile has a partner, the pair stays together for the rest of their lives. However, if one partner dies, the other looks for a new partner.

Finding a territory

A juvenile must find a territory that is not part of the territory of another beaver. A colony of beavers will allow other beavers to pass through its territory, but the colony does not allow them to build lodges there. A beaver marks its territory by making **castor mounds**. It makes castor mounds by piling up mud into **mounds**, or piles, and then rubbing the scent from its castors on the mounds.

A place of its own

A juvenile sniffs each castor mound it passes. The scent of the castor mound tells the juvenile that the territory is **occupied**, or taken. If a territory is occupied, the juvenile keeps moving downstream. When the juvenile finds an area that is not occupied, it makes castor mounds all around the area to mark the territory as its own.

This castor mound tells beavers that the territory is occupied by another beaver.

Building a burrow

As soon as a juvenile has found its territory, it begins making a shelter. A beaver builds a shelter so that it has a place to sleep, escape from harsh weather, and hide from predators. A juvenile without a shelter is at risk of being eaten by predators. A juvenile often makes a **bank burrow** as its first shelter. A bank is land that slopes down into a river or pond. A burrow is an underground home that an animal digs. A juvenile without a partner uses the bank burrow as a shelter until it finds a partner. If it has already found a partner, the juvenile and its partner live in the bank burrow until they finish building a lodge.

If an area is not suitable for a bank burrow, a juvenile may take shelter under a bush or a fallen tree until it finds a partner and builds a lodge.

Bank on it!

A juvenile—or juvenile partners—can make a
bank burrow only if there are **high banks** along
the waterways in its territory. A high bank is an
area of land that rises at least 24 inches (61 cm)
above the surface of the water.

Digging in

To make a bank burrow, a juvenile beaver dives
under water and uses the claws on its front paws
to dig a tunnel into the side of a bank. The beaver
digs inward and upward. Eventually, it reaches
the part of the bank that is above the surface
of the water. When the tunnel is above the
water's surface, the juvenile digs a small
room for sleeping. The beaver may pile
sticks and mud on top of the burrow to
prevent predators from digging down
into the room.

Living in lodges

By summer, most juveniles have partners. The partners need a big home in which to establish their colony. The partners build one of two kinds of lodges—a **bank lodge** or an **island lodge**. A bank lodge is a lodge beavers build against a high bank. An island lodge is a lodge beavers build in the middle of a waterway. The partners build a bank lodge, such as the one shown below, if their territory has high banks. They build an island lodge if their territory has low banks.

Building a lodge

Beaver partners start making a lodge by **felling** trees. The beavers chew the felled trees into smaller branches and logs and then drag them into the water. Carrying the branches and logs between their teeth, the beavers dive to the bottom of the water. They make a pile of branches and logs there. They gather rocks from the bottom of the water and place them on top of the pile of sticks to hold down the sticks. The beavers then dig up mud from around the pile and use it to fill in the spaces between the sticks and the rocks.

Making an entrance

The beavers pile on branches and logs and fill in the spaces until the pile forms a lodge that rises above the surface of the water. They then dive under the water and chew a steep, narrow tunnel from the outside of the lodge toward its center. They also chew a space in the middle of the lodge above the surface of the water. This space is the main living area for the beavers. It is warm and dry. The beavers create at least one more entrance to the lodge.

island lodge

Beaver dams

Beavers build lodges only in deep, slow-moving water. If their habitat has shallow, flowing waterways, such as rivers or streams, beavers build **dams**. A dam is a pile of logs and branches that slows the flow of water in a waterway. The water that flows toward the dam slows down at the dam. The water gets deeper until it forms a pond. When the pond is deep enough, the beavers build a lodge.

Under construction

Beavers build dams in the same way they build lodges—they pile up logs, branches, and rocks and then cover them with mud. Partners can build a dam that is ten yards (9 m) long in less than a week!

Regular repairs

The flow of the water often washes away branches and mud from the dam. Beavers check on their dam every night and make any necessary repairs. They repair the dam by adding branches and more mud to fill in any holes.

Beaver dams slow the movement of water, but they do not block it. Most of the water seeps slowly through the dam or makes its way around the edges of the dam.

Starting a new colony

The juveniles become adults in late autumn or in winter. Adult beavers are able to mate. A female that is ready to mate is in **estrus**. Her body gives off a scent that lets her partner know she is in estrus. The partners mate while swimming under water. The female then becomes **pregnant**. The pregnant female carries embryos inside her body while they **gestate**, or grow and develop. The embryos gestate during winter, for about three months.

Beavers do not have much time in which they can mate. A female beaver may be in estrus for as little as twelve hours a year!

Final preparations

During winter, the beavers stay together in the lodge. They sleep a lot. They also prepare for their kits to be born. The pregnant female makes a soft bed for her kits inside the lodge. She chews twigs until they are soft and stringy and uses them to make the bed. She pulls apart the sticks with her teeth and front paws and covers the floor of the lodge with them.

The kits are coming

When the kits are nearly ready to be born, the father beaver leaves the lodge. He stays in a nearby bank burrow. The mother beaver has her kits alone in the lodge. She places her tail underneath her body. The kits come out of her body and onto her tail. The father returns to the lodge after the kits are born.

Beavers stay warm in their lodges during winter.

Like most rodents, beavers are **herbivores**. Herbivores are animals that eat only plants. In summer, beavers eat the outer bark of trees, as well as **cambium**, which is the soft tissue under the bark. They also eat buds, leaves, and twigs. Berries, roots, and pond plants, such as lilies, are other plant foods that beavers eat.

Snack breaks

Felling a tree is hard work that makes a beaver hungry! After felling a tree, a beaver takes a break to eat. It eats the buds, leaves and twigs from the felled tree. Before they build a lodge or dam, beavers eat most of the buds, leaves, and twigs off the branches they will use as building materials.

26

Surviving cold winters

Most beavers live in parts of the world that have hot summers and cold winters. In winter, the water in some rivers, lakes, and ponds freezes and becomes covered with ice. There are very few plants for beavers to eat at this time of year. Beavers prepare for winter by gathering food. They pile up branches and twigs near one of the lodge's entrance tunnels. The beavers eat these tree parts when food is hard to find in winter.

This beaver is gathering food for winter.

People are the biggest threat to beavers. For hundreds of years, they have trapped beavers for meat and fur. In the 1600s, there were about about 200 million beavers in North America. So many beavers were trapped for the **fur trade**, that the animals nearly became **extinct**. An extinct animal no longer lives on Earth. Today, there are only about 10 million beavers left in North America.

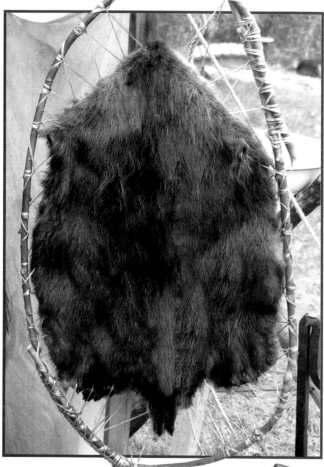

*This picture shows a beaver **pelt**. A pelt is fur that has been removed from an animal.*

The fur trade

European **traders** first arrived in North America in the 1500s. Soon after they arrived, the traders began to trade with Native North Americans. They offered the Native people European goods in exchange for beaver furs. This system of trading was known as the fur trade. The traders sold the furs in Europe, where the furs were made into hats and other clothing. There was a high demand for beaver furs in Europe. The European traders encouraged the Native people to trap more beavers so that more furs could be traded and sent to Europe. As a result, millions of beaver colonies were wiped out.

People problems

Many people like to live near rivers and streams. When beavers build dams, the water sometimes floods onto people's properties and spills over roads. Beavers also fell trees, which upsets some people. It is **illegal**, or against the law, to kill beavers. Some people trap or kill beavers to prevent the animals from building dams, however.

Chemical concerns

Many **chemicals** flow from factories into waterways. Chemicals are poisonous substances that harm people, plants, and animals, including beavers. Beavers that live in waterways that contain chemicals often become sick and die.

Nowhere to go

Some people do not kill or trap beavers, but they try to stop beavers from building dams. People fence off or cover trees so beavers cannot fell them. People also use **pond levelers**, or pipes inserted into beaver dams, as shown above. Pond levelers drain the ponds in which beavers make their lodges. Beavers often leave a habitat if they cannot fell the trees or if their pond is not deep enough. If the beavers cannot find a new habitat in which to live, they die.

Factories make habitats unhealthy for beavers.

Busy beavers

Beavers are important animals. They make **wetland** habitats by creating ponds. Wetland plants, including reeds and grasses, grow in ponds. Many species of birds, insects, and **amphibians**, such as frogs, live in ponds.

Water holders

Ponds are full of water. There is also **ground water** under ponds. Ground water is water that is under the ground. Areas near ponds have a lot of ground water. When an area has a lot of ground water, it does not become dry. All living things need water. By holding water, ponds provide living things with water—even when nearby areas become dry in summer.

This pond habitat was created by beavers.

Clean water

By slowing down the flow of water, beaver dams help **purify**, or clean, the water in streams. As they swirl and flow, fast-flowing streams pick up a lot of **sediment**, or dirt that settles at the bottom of a stream. When a dam blocks a stream, the water slows down. In slow-moving water, a lot of the sediment falls down to the bottom. As a result, the water that trickles through a dam is clean. It contains very little sediment. All living things benefit from clean water.

Get involved!

You can help beavers by supporting **wildlife agencies** that work to save beavers and their habitats. You can also help beavers by reducing **pollution**. Reducing pollution helps keep habitats clean. Another way you can help beavers is by recycling. Recycle paper, plastic, and metal instead of throwing them out. People help all habitats when they cut down on the amount of garbage that they throw out.

Glossary

Note: Boldfaced words that are defined in the text may not appear in the glossary.

amphibian An animal that lives part of its life in water and part of its life on land

backbone A row of bones in the middle of an animal's back

downstream Describing the direction in which a stream or river flows

enamel A hard, protective coating on teeth

estrus The period of time during which a female animal is ready to mate

fell To gnaw at the base of a tree until it falls over

guard hairs The hairs that make up the outer layer of fur on a beaver

oil glands Body parts that produce oil for grooming

partner One of a pair of animals that mate and live together

pollution A substance that is harmful to a habitat

split claw A claw on the hind paw of a beaver that is divided in two

trader A person who buys and sells goods

waterproof Describing something through which water cannot flow

wetland An area of land that is covered with water

wildlife agency A group that works to protect animals and their habitats

Index

Printed in the U.S.A.